Cover Design: Charlton McKinney

JUST MY THOUGHTS
By Siekiem-Kontom
Copyright © 2017
All rights reserved.

Published By:

TEN G PUBLISHING, LLC
NEW YORK, NEW YORK

TABLE OF CONTENTS

Gang Land

Peace and Universal blessings.

This is the topic that I was hesitant to touch on because I have somewhat raw and harsh feelings on this deadly destructive lifestyle. Being born and raised in one of the roughest and most violent neighborhoods in Brooklyn, you become quite numb to certain things.

When I was coming up in my early teens, murder was at its peak in New York City. Not only was it at its peak, many of the people that I passed in the street on a daily basis committed many of these murders. It was common to know someone that "caught a body", also known as one that has murdered someone. These were the older brothers in the neighborhood. The brothers you went to the store for and idolized from a distance, a safe distance.

The irony was that on Monday someone would snatch a mother's pocketbook and on Tuesday help her bring her groceries upstairs. That was Brooklyn, my Brooklyn. A weird paradox of urban culture, crime, and street politics

Reflection...

Growing up I remember faintly about the presence of gangs. Yes, they did exist, just not at today's level. I remember hearing about the Black Spades and Brooklyn's own gang, The Dirty Ones. I remember as a kid being shoved in the building because someone said "The Dirty Ones" were running down our street. I don't know if they were being chased or chasing someone. All I knew is that

4

when they were coming, you had better move out of the way.

I remember the Nation of Gods and Earths being a big thing in the early 80's. Even today they are a crucial part of many communities. For years they have been considered nothing more than a gang. This label was put on the Nation from Government and City officials.

Understand this; ***any belief, religious sect, and organization that does not embrace traditional American values and religious ideals are considered a threat to this establishment.***

Let me say this for the record, I DO NOT consider them a gang or a group of negative people hiding behind their beliefs. In every part of our society, you will find negative individuals from all walks of life and denominations. But to single them out as being other than what they are or were in the community is absurd.

For the most part, the nation rescued many brothers and sisters that were drug addicts and prostitutes. Even though within the Nation there were individuals that weren't full blown righteous, the impact of the Nation had forced many in the community to walk upright and proud. It gave them a sense of pride and direction that many parents, preachers, and teachers could not do.

Present...

Today in New York City the total number of gangs increase on a weekly basis. Out of each known gang there may be several sub divisions of these gangs. Their sole purpose is to base themselves throughout the city to gain control of uncharted territory and monopolize through drug sales, prostitution, gun sales, and extortion.

The gangs of today basically mimic the behavior of America's early immigrants. In the late 1800's, the African-American and Hispanic communities were not the city's problem. The Jewish, Polish, Irish, and Italian communities were the core of the city gangs and illegal activity. A harsh reality is that not only were they part of the heavy illegal activity, they eventually became strong components of the city's financial, judicial and political structure.

Politics as Usual...

Today we have many of the same issues. Different breed of criminals yet the same motive, "Money". Most of us think that these street gangs are just a bunch of reckless fools. On the contrary, many of them are college graduates, ex-service men and women, professionals, and are linked to many public officials. There have even been links to Masonry and other secret fraternities. With this degree of understanding, many individuals use their wit and connections to manipulate the judicial system. There are many founders of various street gangs that were linked to Masonry that used their knowledge and community influence to manipulate naive brothers and sisters.

Exposing them to a world outside their realm of understanding is powerful. Powerful enough to rearrange a person's perception on life itself and the position they play in it. If you were made to believe that an entity could protect you from anything place upon you by man, you may start to think that you're invincible. Many of these individuals that controlled street gangs through their allegiance with certain fraternities were (invincible).

Whether you acknowledge it or not, gangs are the underworld's version of political parties. On the surface we have; Republicans and Democrats, Conservatives and Liberals, etc. In the underworld you have Bloods, Crips, Blackstone Rangers, Latin Kings, etc.

All of these individual gangs represent ideals different from the other just as the different political parties. They hold organized and structured businesses. They have members of their association in Law and Med School.

In the recent years in New York City, the Police and Correctional Department has hired, without knowing, hundreds of active gang members, which created destruction and corruption from within and is becoming a threat to their own infrastructure.

Killing Your Kids...

Parents do not be mistaken, if you suspect that your child is involved in some sought of gang activity, chances are you're right. If you feel that your child is becoming detached from your family structure and leaning more towards the streets, snatch them back. If not, you're killing your kids.

Do not be the foolish parent that walks around stating, "I didn't have a clue". If you are that parent, you're only lying to yourself. If your child out of the blue (no pun intended) begins wearing a lot of red and you don't question this change, you're crazy.

Everyone at this point should know that the color red is the choice color for the gang "Bloods". If you don't believe that your child is actually in a gang, they probably were told to wear that color so they can be identified accordingly because you live in a particular gang affiliated neighborhood. So even if your child is not a Blood, a gang member will tell them to wear that color so that they can identify them as someone from the neighborhood. You as a parent need to know this.

On a whole, this goes for many gangs within the city and abroad. Identifying yourself by a color can save or threaten your child's life. Teenagers are pressured to join gangs by the minute. For whatever reason, they feel that being associated with a gang is a wise decision.

I wonder what is the sales pitch given to these kids, "Hey, either join us or get killed by us, the decision is yours". That is basically the reality many kids are facing. They are being threatened to join a gang for their own safety from the gang.

Teenage females are increasing in numbers in gang affiliation. Yes, there is truth to the stories of females being raped by male gang members for initiation. But what many may not know about is the new wave of females being forced to be involved sexually with other female gang members to join.

8

Whether they are forced to kiss another female or go beyond that point, it is clear that this climate of gang activity is a poison to our communities, and threatening to our very existence.

Media Can Kill...

When the wave of gang violence made its way to New York, the F.C.C. was very clear about their stance on gang related references. Any slang or reference to a gang affiliation was blurted out in various songs. If an artist wore anything gang related it would be digitally distorted, or the video would be taken out of rotation.

That was then; today it's a different ball game. The media realized how big this gang lifestyle actually has become. They are aware that our children are fascinated by some of the recording artists that are openly gang affiliated. Advertisers and manufacturers know that if Snoop Dogg (a known Crip) can sell millions of records, he can also sell millions of sneakers, clothing, food products, etc. They (media) will jeopardize your livelihood for a profit. This is not my opinion, *IT IS FACTUAL TRUTH*.

Why is it important to advertise that Lil Wayne is a Blood? The simple answer is because the major Hip Hop/Music magazines generate revenue off of the controversy that surrounds him. Why do they promote it? Because they know that there is a fascination of this lifestyle in many communities, in this country, and abroad.

We have been tricked to buy into this imagery and these are the negative idols they want "OUR" children to follow. This adds up to millions of dollars for these publication companies.

They inadvertently sell us death. They promote images that destroy our neighborhoods. So that young brother or sister that may want to be an artist, evidently is brought closer to the gang lifestyle through the images that are projected through these magazines.

It is not hard to realize that negativity sells and being positive just gets you by. Known gang members in the music industry have graced more magazine covers than any artist that promotes positive and uplifting messages through their lyrics. Being cognizant of this, we must deal with the fact that our children listen to music and watch T.V. more than they hear our own voices at times. Our influence has become secondary to the views of their favorite artist and neighborhood associates.

The War Report

Brothers and sisters, "there is a war going on outside no one is safe from" (Mobb Deep). The gang violence is sure to get worse before it gets better. Here is something that I will admit; the day will come when all associated with gangs will certainly meet their doom.

The Government works in mysterious ways and when they give the green light it's going to get real nasty out here. If you do not believe me, do your research on how Director

Hoover openly plotted and planned the annihilation of the Black Panther Party.

The extreme difference from the BPP and these misguided gang members is that the Panthers brought change to the hood, and these gangs are bringing about our own self-destruction. The BPP took their complaints and ideas to their local Government and to the White House and defended our civil rights. The gangs that ravage our neighborhoods rape our sisters, kill our brothers, and threaten the future of our generations to follow.

The Government hasn't put real pressure on gangs because they do not threaten this country's economy or political structure. Once this Government feel that gangs are threatening the prosperous future of this country, you better believe that they (gangs) will be systematically eliminated. They will begin with increasing the time gang members are given in prison. Can you imagine someone serving 20 to life for gang related crimes or just being affiliated? Many will come home from prison with lifetime parole.

Depending on the extent of their gang activity, they may never come home, and be placed in prison to serve life sentences from the gate. And I say this not to scare or heighten the fear level in the community. On the contrary, you best believe that whomever the judicial system does not apprehend, armed rebellions will! Law abiding citizens will align themselves to restore order in their communities. If restoring the order means taking the law into their own hands, then you can read in between the lines.

In conclusion, I ask that we take care of each other. We are the greatest species to walk this planet, yet for the most part we conduct ourselves less than human. We should love each other and live within the guidelines of respect and honor.

Everything we do is a part of our history. Just ask yourself 'How will I be remembered? And 'Did I make a difference or did I live a shallow existence?' To all of my people, take care and God bless.

STOP THE GANG VIOLENCE
STOP DOMESTIC VIOLENCE
STOP SEXUAL ASSAULTS
STOP DRUG USE/ABUSE
GET RID OF IGNORANCE
REACH TOWARDS INTELLIGENCE

Striking Back

"The righteous and the wicked can't
occupy the same space at the same
time. One must cease to exist. One must falter"~SK

The words in my quote mean so much. The question at hand today is who shall falter? Are we as a society succumbing to actions of a few evil beings, and if so what are we to do?

I have some strong opinions about the young individuals terrorizing our communities by knocking out and assaulting random people, especially women. I totally feel that every conscious and righteous man including myself is not doing enough about this.

In the African American community, we are slowly evolving into 80% of those whom have developed a **Beast-like** mentality. Leaving 20% of those who want to live a productive and normal life.

These individuals that I refer to with this **Beast-Like** mentality do not see the error of their ways. This city and its sub culture of trivial violence only encourages these perpetrators by not enforcing stronger laws to curb this new wave of destructive behavior. Where is the justice for those unjustly assaulted and victimized? Where does the future of our children lie when punching women in the face is the new celebrated craze?

Where are the community leaders? Where are the activists? Where are the men that are supposed to protect their mothers, sisters and daughters?

JUST MY THOUGHTS

I'm not talking about a 30-minute camera show where community activists show face just to voice out. I'm talking about active and rotating community patrol and watchmen. Where are the OG's of yester-year that reinforced a degree of order in our communities when the police couldn't? Where is the presence of men that proclaim to "rep" their hood while under their watch our brothers and sisters are being randomly assaulted?

I find it amazing that not even the so-called **"THUGS"** have something to say about this. The members of that community are relatively **SILENT**.

The underlying issue is that our judicial system is so wishy washy that committing crimes have become nothing more than games of the street. No one cares about the rules anymore. All that matters are the players, the winners and the losers.

I say let's change the rules of engagement from this point on. I believe if you are caught, arrested and sentenced for these assaults something equally or more damaging should happen to you. For one, the very hand you used to strike these innocent victims should be broken or better yet **CUT OFF**.

Don't squirm or raise your brows to this. At times you have to meet force with equal or more force. Do you know in certain countries males convicted of rape are castrated? Men that steal get their hands cut off. While here in America, the land of the free and home of the brave, a man can kill your parents, rape your children, shoot your cousin and **STILL** stand in court and laugh about it all.

Maybe then after their hands are broken or amputated they will get the message that enough is enough!

Week after week another assault happens to elderly women and unsuspecting teens. What is even more annoying is that once again it is **OUR** community that produces the offspring that acts like they are under a demonic spell.

If it's not our young men wearing their pants with their ass out, they are making all attempts to further submerge our people in chaos. Don't tell me that kids across the country and different races are doing the same thing because that is not the case.

There are no reports of white teens from the Hamptons walking through Bed-Stuy knocking out women and other teens. Nor have you heard any reports about teens from East NY or Bed-Stuy trekking to the Hamptons to pull this crap out there. And if so, you all know what would happen before they even make it to the courthouse.

I tell you my people that this shall not last for long without an uprising of the masses. When that day comes you better pray that your son, nephew, cousin, and brother is on the right side of the track. For the day of reckoning is on its way.

You have been informed!

Blessings.

The Psychology of Violence

Without a doubt in my mind, I can say with no hesitation that (they) want you dead. Now the inquisitive mind will focus on two things in that statement, the words "**they**" and "**dead**".

The fearful will solely focus on the word "**you**". The question that remains unanswered is **WHY? WHY** would someone want you dead? Why would some unknown force want to harm you? Why are you considered disposable?

Here is the answer to the questions you may ask. Simply turn to your closest mirror and take a good look at the image that is you. Look at all of your physical attributes that distinguish you from another. Look at your strengths, weaknesses, your smile, and then look at your devilish grin. It is these images that your society, your world, has conditioned itself to see you as.

Whether you are a clean cut, shaven, well spoken, well-mannered young man, you are a threat to the establishment just as much as the pants sagging foul mouthed young man.

You may simply ask how come? How is this possible? It is possible because whether you are viewed as positive or negative, you're still a threatening force to an establishment that wishes to survive and thrive without your presence? Take a look at our nation's news if you will.

The issues that plague our community are not the world's issues. Say what you will, disagree if you may. To this day the rampant gang violence, gun trafficking through urban cities, and civil misconduct has yet to become cases decided on by the Federal Supreme Court. We are on the lower pendulum of justice. Local municipalities focus on distracting us with handing out fines to young men that sag their pants while Corporate America robs millions out of our retirement, savings, and our health care.

We whitewash our brothers and sisters that have educated themselves, followed their dreams, and have become financially independent. Yet we celebrate buffoonery and those that speak of violence throughout music and videos as if they are the next coming of Christ.

Regardless of **OUR** distorted vision of success, they still want us dead! Ongoing violence in our community has killed more dreams than anything else.

Young people do not dream anymore. They do not see the rainbow as once told to them in storybooks. They see blood, guns, knives, drugs, prostitution and death. When a sub culture is created out of this distorted reality, it gives birth to a future that will perpetuate what they have already learned.

What you now have are communities worldwide that are zombies and driven on violence and social disorder. Now I'm going to ask you a simple question. Is it cheaper and easier to treat the cancer of a society or kill it?

No offense but I have chosen to use cancer to illustrate how serious this problem is to our society and our country as a whole. Look at your community or any community for that matter as the human body. Now look at (cancer) as every other negative image that is used as a stereotype to dehumanize people.

If this cancer entered at the foot of your community, would you wait for it to spread and destroy all that is good and all that is prominent or would you cut off its access to the rest of that body (community)?

This is the same analogy used on a certain demographic of people. People within communities that you and I live in. Communities across this country and world.

So I say to you again, they want you dead! Do not believe that the target is only set for those labeled as hoodlums and thugs. No sir, No ma'am, to my brothers in suits and ties and my sisters in your corporate attire they want you dead as well.

They don't see a utopia with you included in this picture. They don't see you as equal recipients to financial and global freedom regardless of what you have been brainwashed to believe.

Allow me to be very clear, whom I'm referring to has nothing to do with race (particularly). Those that control the world see one color first and that is green. The God they praise is the not the God you and I may praise. Do not get hooked on the Black vs White stigma. This is simply a distraction and is used as a tool to keep the idle mind "idled".

The real issue remains that many brothers and sisters that have become successful in corporate America have risen in rank providing services for companies that drain our community rather than give back to them.

Now this is where the psychology comes in. We are conditioned to be robbed by a familiar face rather than one we see as a stranger to the community. If you didn't understand that analogy I will explain further.

They will set up a table on the busiest street in your community handing out reasonably rated cell phones for low income residents. All they need is your address, social security # and other pertinent info. They will hand out these cell phones quicker than condoms at bachelor party.

Oddly enough no one would even ask them where their personal info is going and what will it be used for. Many will claim the info gathered is not to verify credit worthiness so why do they need it? Well for those that don't know, that info is used to gather Intel on you and everyone you call on that phone.

You see, President Bush revised a little act called the Privacy Act, which is monitored by the government. A government-sponsored program backs the phones that everyone was so happy to get from the brother in the suit. DUH! So even if you can't afford the triple play at home they can monitor you through their government issued phones. I know I may have drifted off track but I must to get back to the point I'm making which is, they want you dead!

We must always remember that warfare is **MENTAL**. My people this is only part one of my installment "The psychology of violence". Be sure to stay tuned for part two. Until then, stay **ALERT**, **JUST** and **TRUE**.

Take care and God Bless.

JUST MY THOUGHTS

A View from My Eyes

This time around I will share my views on Politics, Power, and Principles. Three key elements or sub components that make up the nucleus of our society at large.

Pol'i-tic (pol'i-tik) 1. Political: as' the body politic. 2. Sagacious in promoting a policy; prudent; in a bad sense, artful; cunning.

How exact is this definition? I would say cunning, artful, and prudent in a bad sense. Is it safe to say that politics and trickery go somewhat hand-in-hand? Upon observation it looks like a Vail that gracefully overlies the other, both acting in concert with another. Since my interest with the world of politics, I have come to know that those that dare to step into this arena must be as ruthless as they are righteous and it's a clear contradiction, yet necessary.

The only way to implement decent policies and orders is to go against opposition and defeat them by any and all means. Government and its sub divisions are structured to **control**, not to incorporate independent thoughts for a unified nation. They are specifically there to suppress the minority views and convert them into the ideologies of their oppressors.

The majority of this country is living close to or under the poverty line. Universal health care should be a top priority for our nation because a healthier nation in turn means a healthier and more productive work force.

What most of the general public doesn't realize is that IT techs, C.E.O's, and Middle America are not the overwhelming majority without sufficient healthcare. On the contrary, those without sufficient medical insurance are usually the laborers, entry-level employees, unemployed and those on government assistance. Even though they make up the majority of this country's work force, their occupations are not the source of this nation's wealth.

We have moved away from the industrial revolution and billions of dollars are now made from the click of a computer. The money isn't in drilling for oil, it's in the **selling** of it!

When in regards to politics, it's all the same. In order for this country to respect and acknowledge your views and worth, you must illustrate that you are the lifeline of this nation. You must show that you represent the voices that can tilt the structure and global relations of this nation.

Pow'er (-er), 1. Ability to act; faculty of doing or performing something. 2. Extended energy; vigor; force. 3. Control; authority; influence

Power. Everyone to some degree actually believes that we have some. The highest degree of understanding is realizing that you and I have NO control of what we believe is our power.

Power, my friends, is only a state of mind. Only to be as strong as your opposition is weak. There is a saying that "Power respects Power", well that is only in the regards to war. The strong respect the strong for each side know defeat will not be easy. Their very existence is threatened, a chance either side doesn't want to succumb to. Power respect power, are you sure of that?

The highest degree of power to me is God. Do you think that there can be two Gods? Which one would you follow, which one would you believe? The path of righteousness is by the way God. If two different people chose to follow their God's path to it, who will actually reach it? Power is **Control**! Power is energy that if harnessed and used wisely. Great minds can become brilliant minds. In order for that to happen, you must accept that power is not defined by what you have conquered but knowing that you are capable of conquering any and everything. That, my friend, is **POWER!**

Prin-ci-ple, 1. The fundamental law or truth upon which others are based; a moral standard.

The foundation. The very thing that distinguishes men from boys and women from girls. Not based on age but on a degree of maturity and an over-standing of life and what it entails. No one person's principles are greater than the next, the measure can only be determined by the circumstances in one's life.

A husband and father's principles may differ from a young man without children. This does not mean that the young man's principles are less relevant, they are held in different regards to no fault of his own. His sacrifices and obligations are simply not the same.

Principles align us with spirituality and morality. It is the outline that defines who we are and what we will or will not do. To embrace principles one must embrace a true sense of morality and order, knowing that everything has its place.

One must categorize what is important to he/she and to what extent, and carry them out accordingly. We raise our children according to our principles, setting them up with guidelines for their future. This will provide them the opportunity to make wise and sound judgements, and putting priority over pleasures.

What we embrace as important to us determines what we put out to the universe (energy). When we live a life structured on morals we conduct ourselves in a positive and upright sense. We respect the laws of nature and abide by a standard that can be only beneficial to our well being.

Living in a country with those of different religions and cultures, we learn that principles are fundamental to each person's existence. Some sacrifice their lives over their principles, while others have a disregard for life because of their lack of. We exist in a time where morality and integrity has taken a back seat to greed and selfishness.

In order to live in this world free of its imperfections, you must consciously live "outside" of this world. One must live outside the hype, falsehoods, and negativity. We as people must determine what is important to us and our existence.

Living without boundaries is the beginning of one's own end.

Take care and God bless.

A State of Emergency

Allow me to vent, just a little. Allow me to say some things that I feel need to be said. Give me your undivided attention while I touch on a few issues. Ladies and gents, these are just my thoughts.

For starters, I am becoming extremely disgusted with the behavior and mind state of some of our young brothers. There is a deadly train of thought that has captured their soul. A cloud of confusion that prevents them from acknowledging their worth. It has become somewhat of a fad to carry themselves unkempt, dirty, poorly groomed, and disrespectful. The era of a man's man is dying in the hands of this lost generation.

There is nothing noble about being a young man of little substance. Men aren't born men, they are groomed with poise, respect, and obedience as a youth. Those that have not had these influences, and those that have chose to ignore them are the center of our destruction.

You, the young men that have little to no regards for life. **You** are the reason young innocent men die by the hands of reckless fools. **You**, the young men that lie and steal are the reason it is hard for hard working brothers to walk through their own neighborhood without being harassed.

You, the young men that have turned a red or blue tee into colors of war. **You** are responsible for the deaths of many innocent and vibrant lives across this country.

Heartless fools imitating acts of Hollywood hoodlum theatrics. Making yourself appear stronger and bolder than **you** actually are. But what you fail to realize is that when that movie ends, that multi-millionaire actor goes home. **You** are the one stuck in the facade of a character that has ridden **you** of your own essence.

I am tired of seeing young men disrespect young women. It is clear that some young women find humor in this type of behavior. I am confused how women that are addressed as bitches respond in glee. When did sisters give up on sisterhood?

Young women that do not set a tone of respect open a door for disrespect. I constantly see young woman destroy every ounce of womanhood by exploiting themselves through sex and fashion.

This society has convinced young teens that exposing your body earns you the attention of an adult. This society tells young woman that sex sells. It is quite hard to dispute when many products being sold today are marketed with a sexual undertone. If you want a pair of jeans, some young sister is posing spread out on top of a brother with nothing on but those jeans.

If you want a beer, there is a bikini clad woman gyrating with a beer in her hand as if it has given her an orgasm. These are the images our sisters are seeing. They are the same images your daughters, nieces, and cousins equate with being a "woman".

There is a break down in our community and society as a whole. Teenage pregnancy, sexual transmitted diseases, adolescent prostitution, and teenage drug abuse are all key elements of this destructive lifestyle. We are living in a time where these young woman actually think being exploited sexually means acceptance and love from their male counterparts.

Who began with this way of thinking? Who continues to allow this behavior to transpire, and where does it end? If we do not address it, we are ignoring it. What some people think are harmless acts of finding one's self, others consider as a road to nowhere. Allowing our future to drift away to a life without purpose is equivalent to witnessing a suicide.

As adults of sound mind, we have the responsibility to educate and provide a better understanding of life to those that do not. To our women; for every female that you see out of control without your intervention is another girl lost. To our men; for every young man that we see carrying himself in a sub-human state without our intervention, we are setting him and other young brothers up for absolute destruction. We do not succeed as a people if we consciously allow one of us to deliberately fail. One for all, and all for one.

Take care and God bless.

Why Do We Fall Apart?

During my brief hiatus I took a long and thorough look at my community and the beautiful people that keep it up and going strong. Despite the negative press and stigma that many inner city neighborhoods are plagued with, we always shine and rise to greatness.

It is no wonder why Bed-Stuy, which was one of highest ranking areas in Brooklyn in murders is now the new cultural hot spot. Times have changed, people have evolved, and money always talks that talk.

I call this "Rebuilding the Broken Wall" because this is what we're all trying to do within this society we live in. *We are in a state of repair.* We have to take our resources to make a better way for those to follow.

"Why Do We Fall Apart" expounds on the question of what causes the weakening within our community. The broken wall is symbolism for the men, women and children. Individuals that have been taken out of their natural state of being Fathers, Mothers, Brothers and Sisters, and reduced to enemies and non-compassionate people.
Why do we fall apart?

When you live a community where jobs are few and crime is common, it does something ill to the will of a man. If one decent job comes to the area, the hunger for survival comes out and turns most into competitors.

This Darwin type of behavior begins to overshadow the ideals of love for humanity. Survival by any means is paramount to all in this redefined realm of humanity.

Where does desperation begin? Does it begin with the

heinous acts of violence in the world around us? Does it begin in the hearts of the desolate, hungry, and ignored? Wherever it begins, its roots are the breakdown of morality and ethics within one's society. When visualizing about being successful takes a back seat to actually devising a scheme to gain profits, illicitly and being corrupt, we have indeed fallen apart.

Where did we fall apart?

Today it's Society vs. Man. The world that we have created has turned on us and is eating us alive, right down to the core of our own existence. We have become pawns in our own game. **How do we ever rebuild this broken wall?** We live to die, we work to survive, we fight to win, but when do we live to love?

It seems that the only time we show love to our fellow brothers and sisters is when something of value is attached to it. Millions of dollars are donated to assist victims in natural disasters. If the contributors were told that they couldn't write a dime of that money off in taxes, would they consider donating again? Would they part with money to benefit the less fortunate even if their names weren't acknowledged? Are we a society that lends a hand for the love of humanity or notoriety?

If all charitable deeds went unrecognized and unappreciated, would we have so many charities within this country at all? If I gave a homeless person $5.00 and he turned around and stole $10.00 worth of food, would I help another person in that same situation? Is man's need for survival greater than our need to give? Is the amount of our charity only measured by the crisis in front of us?

Those are questions that we all must answer. Regardless of the answer, the answer is our reality. Whether it's good or bad, it is the reality that **WE** have created.

To rebuild that broken wall we must rebuild ourselves. We must step out of the hype and back into the light. We are a divine species of infinite possibilities. Harnessing our true and god given capabilities will bring forth a love that man has yet to see.

My people, in order to rebuild we must destroy. Destroy everything that is negative, false and poisonous to our well being.

My people, take care and God bless.

JUST MY THOUGHTS

If You Love Your Hood

How many times can a person be tired of being "sick and tired"? Or fed up with the never ending nonsense that has plagued our communities? I'm speaking of **GUN** violence, **GANG** activity, and **DRUGS.**

We have developed this warped mind state that forces us to speak under our breath about the crimes against humanity in our own neighborhood. We watch the attention and hype increase about Occupy Wall Street while we have forgotten about our own Streets.

We have become blind to the fact that every life that is taken by gun fire increases our own probability of facing the same demise.

We think these events are isolated occurrences. How is it that they keep happening to the same demographic of people in primarily the same communities across the nation? Let's keep it real. I haven't heard about other ethnic groups involved in gang violence to this extent in this city. Incidents that have occurred in other communities are so far and few in between that it barely even makes the news.

Yet, **WE**, in the African/Caribbean/Latino and many other brown communities at large conduct ourselves as if we have a license to kill at will?

There was a recent tragedy (2011) that took the life of Zurana Horton 33, a mother of 12 in a meaningless crime that took NYC to a new low. This young lady lost her life shielding children as she walked home from a neighborhood school with her own children. Horton is said to have been killed by shots that came from a rooftop of a nearby apartment complex.

The results of this shooting is just another tragic page in the history books of NYC. Let's not be confused here; there are many Zurana Horton's across the nation. Taking the life of innocent people has become a way of life for heartless and mindless individuals.

My people, you want me to be honest with you then I will. I feel that those responsible shouldn't be afforded the rights of the judicial system. I believe that they should be dealt with in the same accord as they chose to handle their business.

There is saying "Live by the gun, die by the gun" If you choose to live your life according to that path then you should accept and be prepared for whatever comes with it. This liberal way of living and philosophy in NYC gives hardened criminals a pass to hurt and murder innocent people, live to talk about it, and do interviews and write books which in turn makes them into hood celebrities.

That woman's blood stains the sidewalk while more senseless crimes will continue to occur on that same corner. Cowards took a mother's life and we as a community say nothing in protest to the quality of life that we live in. We do not care unless it happens on our street, and even then many of you complain behind closed doors. In an uproar you will scorn the police department for not doing enough while **YOU will say and do NOTHING!**

This way of thinking and operating is very psychological. We have been conditioned to give away our own power and look for leadership in others. This is why as a community we are victims to our own neglect. We do not know how to save ourselves.

We are need of a serious awakening. We are expiring at large amounts and it plays out in the media as nothing out of the norm.

This country and local municipalities care little to nothing about these gang wars that ravage our communities. They know that all of these gangs threaten nothing of importance in the overall infrastructure of government and finance so until it affects **THEIR** community **NOTHING** will be done.

For all of you gang members, if you want to do something for the history books then build some houses for the homeless or put someone's kid through college so they can make a difference in the community from which they came. If you want to take it to another level, bring all of the pedophiles, rapist, and murderers to justice.

CLEAN UP OUR COMMUNITY INSTEAD OF DESTROYING IT!

There comes a point in life when one must be accountable for his/her actions and the energy they bring forth into existence. If one does not take responsibility for their actions, they leave the fate of their lives to be dealt with and orchestrated by another. When this happens, you have little to no control over what is about to take place. At that moment my friend be assured that this is the **END** of you.

My people, do the knowledge and take care of each other. Blessings.

Help Wanted: Thinkers

I'm still on vacation but I decided to drop back in for a moment to shed some light on an increasingly dim situation. Over the past few months I've noticed a lack in presence of public officials around town. Everyone seems to be in hiding, trying clean their hard drive of porn and self taken pictures of them flexing in the mirror. You would think that these were the antics of a teenager and not our elected officials.

So I pose the question, where are the thinkers? Where are the intellectuals that discuss the climate of our current state of being? It appears to me that everyone has taken off their thinking caps for a little fun in the sun.

A break is entitled to everyone at some point and time, but where does that leave the people that depend on insight and information from others? Well, it means that they are actually going to have to think for themselves. They are going to have to look out of their windows and scream at injustice in their **OWN** voice. They are going to have to speak up and out with their convictions and stop hiding behind the signature of "Anonymous".

When community leaders are in the forefront, everyone has an opinion or gripe. When they are out of town or too busy, the community itself remains quiet. No one person addresses issues or demands answers for the injustice that plagues our communities. They sit and wait for the Calvary. Some individuals won't or better yet can't steer you in the right direction because they have become content with being a follower, a listener, and not a thinker!

It would be unfair of me to say that every community or group of individuals within a community are like this. I will say this, many of you probably wouldn't complain about an issue that threatens your way of life unless 50 others complained along side you. Many sit back and let an outsider of their community decide what is best for them instead of taking charge of their own community issues.

We associate "Action with Thinking" and many of us do not want to think, we just want results. We don't want to know what it takes to have the municipality come out and fix the pot holes in our streets, we just want them fixed. We do not want to go to our state's capital and lobby for more funding for our communities, we just want more funding for after school, daycare, and senior centers.

When we don't receive what we want, only then do we bang down the doors of a councilmen or councilwoman and put on our angry face for television.

Are you a philosopher?

Having the ability and capability to rationalize and organize a constructive thought is a gift within itself. We have taken the gift of "Thinking" as a burden. No one wants the responsibility of being relied on or accountable for their thoughts or their actions that follow their thoughts.

We are the "Active-Inactive", a terminology that I created for those that appear to be doing a lot but actually are doing nothing. The terminology is equivalent to a Police Officer that walks on the beat but never addresses issues he/she sees or make any arrest. A Doctor that walks the hospital halls in scrubs but always refuses to speak to their patients or stand in surgeries. A politician in expensive clothing that only goes into their community office to check their voicemails and charge their IPHONES.

Sadly these are the people we leave our thinking up to.

34

I was told as a child that everyone should know a little about everything. Do not leave your source of knowledge up to one person. When you give up your God given ability to think you surrender more of yourself than actually know.

You become feeble in your thoughts and actions, becoming easier to control. This is how governments rule. This is how and why we elect representatives to speak for us. We give power away to one person and it takes the responsibility out of our hands. When they fail we blame them, we don't see it as a collective issue. It's like saying "I sent YOU out to do it, so YOU failed not ME!"

My people, the purpose for me writing this is to remind us all of our responsibility as **Human Beings**. We have an obligation to our creator to be vital and productive. Each person has a value that cannot be measured by any monetary amount. We are bestowed with powers that are limitless and these powers are harnessed through the wonderful gift called our "MIND"

*TIPS FOR ALL:

-Remove your CD and DVD library for an actual book library.

-Expose yourself to something that you generally wouldn't do. If you like R&B concerts consider going to a Jazz or an Opera concert.

-Watch programing that actually teaches you something that you didn't know.

-Venture out to Book readings and lectures.

-Invest more family time at museums and public libraries.

-Allow your kids to ask questions, telling them to be quiet is not encouraging them to think freely.

-Last but not least, live your life with a purpose. If there is nothing that stimulates you then cannot stimulate the world around "YOU". A person with a purpose is not just breathing, they are LIVING.

Take care and God Bless.

The World As I See It

Being one who loves to put my thoughts onto to paper, I have been quite under the radar lately. That is not to say that I've dropped the ball on any of my initiatives or concerns. I've been taking the world in as it evolves and revolves, watching from the eye of the storm as we spiral into the next chapter.

I use the term (chapter) to embody the thought and phrase "Book of Life" because this in which we call life has many chapters and stages in which we go through in order to evolve.

Our thoughts and behavior continuously creates situations and circumstances for us to learn from on a daily basis. Over a period of time I have gone through some remarkable changes. I say remarkable because it's amazing to acknowledge your own growth, faults, and obstacles and to be able to learn from and build off of them.

With that being said I can only share my thoughts of the world as I see it. I embody a true concern for the outlook of our future, community, and world.

JUSTICE: 1). Just or right action or treatment. JUDGE. The carrying out of law. The quality of being fair or just.

We are all familiar with the word justice but how many of you are familiar with its definition? How many of us can say that we are the recipients of justice?

I can recall not too long ago the execution of a man by the name of Troy Davis. It was an execution to be considered an unjust fate decided by the Georgia Judicial System and Supreme Court.

For starters I must admit that I had not reviewed the transcripts of that case in its entirety nor do I claim to know all of the evidence provided. What I do know within myself is that there is a practice of discriminatory proceedings involved in the execution of Death Row inmates.

I am not an advocate for the Death Penalty, nor will I stand in solidarity with the ones who have admitted their guilt and is set to be executed. What I will do is shed light on the Death Row inmates that have admitted to committing their crimes and their lives have been spared. Inmates that have 90% or more evidence to associate them with the crime and yet they are given the opportunity to see the sun rise yet another morning. When we can execute a person without evidence, DNA, or an admission of guilt then what are we doing people?

What we are doing is abusing our appointed power by man. Not power given from our God, The Most High. God has not given man that authority to make judgement calls on another's life. And for this, we all bear the burden of the outcome of a man's life expiring. We all felt that pain and it is not a good feeling. We have lost control of our will to be HUMAN and embrace our feelings and concern for humanity. We have become numb and distracted from our true essence while ignoring all that is righteous and just.

In the years to come we as a nation will face again the issue of salvation vs. slaughter. The question that resonates is what side of the fence we will play. Will we become consumed and driven by a world of torture? Or will we STOP, THINK, and DECIDE how to evolve as a people of logic, reasoning, facts, truth, and JUSTICE for ALL?

Take care and God bless.

F*%& Your Feelings

Some may find irony in my greetings when the basis of this pamphlet is to ruffle a few feathers. Do note that my intentions are not to create chaos but to put an end to it. Too many walk around believing their own hype. Misleading my people, misdirecting and ill informing those around them.

Allow me if you will to speak my peace and set things straight. If you feel that you may have an issue with what is to follow then F*%& "YOUR" feelings as well!

Now where should I begin? Oh yes, Black Leadership! I have so much to say about you. For one you have become the most sensationalized, fame driven, egotistical, no balls having, bi-partisan, turn the cheek to get kicked on the other side of your face- movement.

Black leadership in Amerikkka simply means make some African Americans appear important. So when shit goes wrong we can use them as an example to claim that Amerikkka have accepted us into its society and culture.

Blacks, I mean **unarmed blacks**, have been shot and murdered by citizens and law enforcement at alarming rates. Under the Presidency of Obama and a Congress of more African Americans in history, no one can seem to properly address the disdain in this nation against African Americans. Honestly I do not place blame on the government.

I place the blame on this nation of complacent Negroes that still have that syndrome of waiting for someone to speak for them and heal them. Shit continuously happens to African Americans in this country simply because we allow it to.

Secondly, because spineless African Americans have been elected into our local branches of government to keep us calm and convince us that change is on the horizon. All I have to say about that is NEGUS PLEASE! Every year a Black person that is unjustly and heinously killed only brings attention to these politicians' platforms. Where are the changes in the law? Where are the repeals in the gun law that makes it illegal to shoot an unarmed person? Where has the protection for the average citizen gone? I see so much street activism taking place that one would believe that someone in office must be listening to the cries of the people.

Unfortunately for us in the community they are not. I continue to see and hear about more rapes and gang violence in our communities than arrests. I read about and witness more of our Black politicians going to jail for under the table deals and scams than I see them getting persecuted for going against the grain and actually giving an "eff" about the communities and people they are supposed to represent. Are they merely driven for fame or did they come to make a CHANGE?

Are we the fools for consequently relinquishing our voice and power to these Black leaders when they are leading us nowhere fast? You're damn right we are.

Gang Violence/Members- How shall I put this, well you all are simply PUSSY! From my over standing, the ideology behind "gangs" were to protect the community from outsiders of that community.

They protected the elders and property from being robbed and burglarized. They prevented unwarranted attacks from the police and such. Today gang members cut faces, shoot people, assault women and rape them.

Day after day a gang assault happens yet when the police are out here holding court on our innocent brothers and sisters I never see gang members mobilizing. I just don't see you cats!!!

The sad shit about this is that most of you gang members have a limited life span and you don't even know it. You dumb motherfuckers walk around well off into your 30's really thinking that people are scared of you. Fool, we are laughing at you. We are praying for you. We are hoping you do not procreate and bring an innocent baby into this world that may be killed by a bullet meant for you.

Exactly what will it take for you to realize that this nation has a plan for you? A plan that leads to your demise. This craze has taken such a drastic shift to the left it has now claimed the souls of teenage females leaving parents bewildered. Our young ladies have given up lip gloss for sticks and knives. Over the past years female gangs have attacked people on the transit system to innocent women sitting in the park.

I can recall a disgraceful attack of a young teen female in a Brooklyn, NY McDonald's by six teen females. This brutal attack was captured on a cell phone and shared through social media, which consequently lead to the arrest of these reckless and lost teenagers.

The female dynamic in gangs have always existed. Their rise in numbers and severity of attacks over the years have even surprised their male counterparts. Our brothers and sisters have been brainwashed. They have been conditioned to see no further than their immediately reality. A reality that has been designed by another and orchestrated throughout media and sensationalized through music and film as nothing more than fame through fighting, fucking, and fabricating lies of a life yet to be obtained.

This culture has created a nation of sleep walkers. Keep sleep walking and you shall permanently sleep before you have the chance to see the error of your ways. **WAKE THE EFF UP!**

Political/Social THOTS- You thought I was going to let you slide by without getting at you? How naive of you. You all know the type of women I am referring to. The type that throw you the pussy because they want to be seen with someone of substance, purpose, and position. The women that don't give two shits about the state of the community but is always smiling in a politician's face. The women that will do anything including shining an official's shoes with her dress. STOP IT!

Event after event I have been to with women, with their titties hanging out, tight, improper clothing, acting as if they are concerned about the community when all they really want to do is "eff". Now you may ask where does he get this from? How does he know this to be true? Well it is because I have "effed" some of them. See, don't be up in my face trying to blow smoke acting like you are down for the cause when all you want to do is drop your draws. The sad thing is those I didn't "eff" are mad that I didn't. I guess you can't use my name in a slanderous conversation.

Here is the thing, if you are not bringing anything to the table then sit your lame ass down. If you are not about creating change then stop trying to lean on men who are. Stop trying to piggy back your way to the top. Get off your knees and stand tall.

There are so many women in politics and community outreach that actually give a damn. These women are about making a difference and creating initiatives to empower other women and the community on the whole. These are the women you should pay attention to and link up with.

Stop associating with the women that are not involved in community affairs but break their neck for tickets to Black Tie Affairs in search of a politician or Advocate to rub elbows with and possibly their breast. Stop being sensationalized by shows like Scandal. Women have so much more to offer than being a bed warmer or social arm piece.

Ladies- HAVE SOME GODDAMN DIGNITY.

Racism- if the masses do not know by now, allow me to put you on notice. I do not give an "eff" about racists nor the systemic concept of racism. I am aware that it does exist in every walk of this society. What supersedes their (racists) existence in my circumference is my direct connection to the Most High, God, and a firm sense of knowledge of self.

See many Black people feel inferior in the room filled with predominantly white people and other nationalities because you have been conditioned since a child to fear them and the unknown. I, on the other hand was raised with a sense of pride that only the fretful and stand-offish racist can only describe as arrogance. I am not arrogant. I am educated and in tune with the bullshit racists attempt to scare my people with.

Most of you so called proud Black people mentally submit to whites and others to show them that you are capable of assimilating and getting along with them. Many Blacks fail to realize is that racism is a concept embodied not only by the white population. Every nationality has demonstrated a degree of racism towards the Black population on this planet. Do not be foolish to believe they (whites) own the exclusive rights to racism.

Gandhi, the man of peace was a racist and have expressed negative views on the African in various quotes. Many cultures including Latin and Caribbean have exhibited acts of racism against the African American and African for that matter. Leaving the African American confused and lost within their own identity.

Despite of the treatment from other cultures, if you are not being genuine and true to yourself then they are not getting to know the true you. They are witnessing the person who disguises who they are at heart just to fit in and socially thrive. They are getting to know the slave in you.

I have nothing against white people or any other nationality. With that being said, in their presence I shall never present myself to be sub human, less educated, less informed nor less culturally and socially aware of the state of my people in this nation and abroad. When you see me you see GOD, not a nigger or some infantile being clinging for my life on the heels of another.

The concept of "racism" is so bizarre because to oppose it one must give it so much energy and time simply to denounce it. What I prefer to do is just live a righteous and just life. The world and its people can judge me by my actions and character. It may sound cliché but it is true, a man's character is the true definition of who he is.

Regardless of your hue or ethnicity. If you are an ass then you are an ass. Being Black does not make you a greater ass nor makes the threat more intense. Society has forced you to see the Black community in this light. Sadly enough many Blacks prefer to be viewed as a larger than life thugs until the bullets from the gun of a scared white man rips through them. Go figure! Then we are thrown into this race war and struggle between ones identity. Is Black an identity or perception?

Are Blacks threatening or is the world around us threatened by our mere existence? So we may all ask ourselves, how do we rid the world of racism and the racist? My answer to that is to carry yourself with dignity and pride and see the next person in the way. Treat your fellow brother and sister as you would want to be treated. Allow people to be who they are and not alter who you are simply to get along or fit it. **No one respects a fraud on any level. REMEMBER THAT.**

Now this may have offended some and if you truly know me then you know that I do not care. I told you in the title "Eff your feelings". Till next time. Yes. There will definitely be a next time.

Blessings.

ABOUT THE AUTHOR

Siekiem-Kontom is a Brooklyn, NY native and advocate. The founder of MSKM PRESENTS (a community foundation) best known for his many initiatives including GIVING BACK TO HELP OTHERS GET AHEAD and FINDING YOUR FUTURE SCHOLARSHIP FUND.

Born and raised in Bedford-Stuyvesant and a 19 year veteran with the NYC Dept. of Correction, he illustrates a candid perspective of the dual reality he faces daily by being a citizen and an Officer.

With a passion for setting the record straight, Siekiem-Kontom gives you a view of our society and it's sub-culture in a way that only he can.

With 11 years of community service, mentoring, and public speaking, Siekiem-Kontom has compiled the grit, pain and truth within his world. Here he shares only a glimpse in "Just My Thoughts"

Contact Information
siekiemkontom0513@gmail.com
www.about.me/mskm_presents

DEDICATION

To my mother, Barbara Jean-Russell McKinney, rest in peace. It is because of you that I write these words. It was you that raised me to be inquisitive, outspoken and fearless but most importantly compassionate towards my fellow brother and sister.

To my beloved children, Ieszan Siekiem-Kontom McKinney and Isis Syleen Kontom-McKinney, use my words and insight to navigate through this thing called life.

To my father, Dr. Reverend Michael A.H. McKinney, thank you for instilling in me the desire to make a change in this world through my actions and words.

To my sister, Daphanie Ann, rest in peace.

To my nieces and nephews, Ty-Ty, Dominique, Donte, Te'ana, and Joel, I love you. May the Most High continue to guide you.

To my brother's, Charlton & Kyle McKinney, thank you for always having my back.

To my sister Stephanie Turner, thank you for your unconditional love and support.

SPECIAL THANKS & SHOUTOUTS

To the elders of N.A. ROCK, BED-STUY, thank you for guiding me throughout my teen and adult life.

To my co-workers and supervisors at the NYCDOC, may you continue to stay upright and safe.

To the Nation of the Gods & Earths, life has taught me that learning the 120 was essential to my existence. Peace be unto you.

One love to the inner circle: Rasheen, Frederick, Wise, Anthony, Lee, Infinite, Shawn (Black), Derrick, T. Crawford, Miz, Murdock (RIP), Born, Ty-Quan, Cire, and L.C.

To all of my people in the fight to eradicate injustice, **STAY VIGILANT.**

Made in the USA
Middletown, DE
31 March 2021